Mr. Boomsma's Substitute Teacher Workbook

Walter Boomsma

Copyright 2013, 2015, 2016, 2019 by Walter Boomsma

All rights reserved. No part of this book may be reproduced in any form or by any electronic or mechanical means including information storage and retrieval systems—except in the case of brief quotations embodied in critical articles or reviews without permission.

For information address Walter Boomsma, Abbot Village Press, 17 River Road, Abbot ME 04406

http://AbbotVillagePress.com

This publication is designed to provide accurate and authoritative information in regard to the subject matter covered. It is sold with the understanding that the publisher and author are not engaged in rendering legal, accounting, or other professional service. If legal advice or other expert assistance is required, the services of a competent professional person should be sought.

--From a Declaration of Principles Jointly Adopted by a Committee of the American Bar Association and a Committee of Publishers and Associations.

First Edition August 2013

Second Edition March 2015

Third Edition September 2019

Some illustrations by Presenter Media, licensed to Walter Boomsma

PresenterMedia.com

4416 S Technology Drive

Sioux Falls SD 57106 USA

ISBN-13: 978-1-950945-01-6

Printed in the United States of America

Table of Contents

About this workbook 3

Welcome… 5

    Note-taking suggestions: 5

    Your instructor's expectations for today's workshop 6

    Your expectations for today's workshop 6

Module One - A day in the life of a professional substitute 7

    Managing expectations 7

    The professional substitute's checklist 7

    The professional substitute's "sub-pack" 8

Module Two - Classroom management 9

    Principle one - behavior is largely a product of its immediate environment ... 9

    Principle two – behavior is strengthened or weakened by its consequences ... 9

    Principle three – Behavior responds better to positive than negative consequences ... 9

    Principle four –The future determines whether a behavior has been punished or reinforced. ... 9

    Skill #1 – Getting and keeping students on task 11

    Skill #2 – Maintaining a high rate of positive teacher/student interactions ... 12

    Skill #3 – Teaching expectations 12

    Skill #4 – Responding non-coercively 12

    Skill #5 – Avoiding traps 12

    Other management tips 13

Module Three -- Legal considerations and special education 15

    General legal aspects 15

    Small-town Maine = big-time liability 15

    Safe schools 17

    First aid and safety—medications 17

    Child abuse reporting 17

    Sexual harassment 17

    Evacuations, assemblies, field trips, etc. 18

    Suicide awareness and prevention 18

Special education 18
Module Four -- Teaching Strategies 21
How we learn 21
KWL charts 22
Cooperative learning 22
Questioning 23
Activity for the teaching strategies module 24
Module Five -- Action Planning 25
Resources for further study 27
Websites 27
Websites specific to Special Education 28
A Substitute's Checklist 29
Sample Lesson Plan 31
"Johnny hit me!"-- a case study 35
Questions and Answers 37
Bibliography 39
About the Instructor 39
Books by "Mr. Boomsma" 40

About this workbook

This book was developed for use in "Mr. Boomsma's Substitute Teacher Workshop" and, as such may appear to be missing content if viewed without participating. However, there is a fair amount of standalone information and valuable resources. It should further be noted that some of the information such as the process for fingerprinting and background checks is specific to the State of Maine. Regulations and processes may differ widely among states and school districts.

At the time of writing, the Substitute Teacher Workshop is currently offered by three Adult Education Programs. Additional information is available at http://wboomsma.com.

Welcome...

I have a past that is rich in memories. I have a present that is challenging, adventurous and fun because I am allowed to spend my days with the future. I am a teacher.

Sir Kenneth Robinson, noted English author, speaker, and education advisor says that if we want to discover what the future is like we should spend some time with Kindergartener teachers.

At least one study suggests that every student who completes twelve years of public education will spend at least the equivalent of one full school year with substitute teachers.

Those two observations suggest that the career you are in or considering is one of great opportunity and impact. I hope you leave today's workshop energized and challenged, but also a bit frightened.

Becoming a substitute teacher is not an event—it's a process. And it's a lifelong process at that. The teacher you are replacing for the day has likely had a minimum of four years of college, completed a student teaching internship, and attended unnumbered professional development programs. He or she is generally in the same classroom every day with the same kids and is able to make plans ahead.

When you walk into that same classroom, you've likely had less than seven hours of formal training. You don't know the kids. For that matter, you don't even know where basic supplies and materials are kept. And yet you are challenged to substitute for the permanent teacher.

Today's class is designed to help you feel somewhat prepared and, at the same time, challenge you to remember that the best learners make the best teachers. As your confidence grows, you'll find that your enjoyment also increases. Your task is challenging, adventurous and fun because you are gaining the right to spend your days with the future. You are a teacher.

Note-taking suggestions:

This workbook follows today's program outline and allows you to take notes. Some notes you may wish to make:

1. Questions – While we will be attempting to answer most questions, you may find ideas or questions you'll want to make a note of and research later.
2. Reading – Note references and topics that you want to follow up with additional reading.
3. Recall – The traditional reason for making notes is to record or note points that you want to focus on remembering.
4. Reflection – Some areas you'll find yourself just wanting to "think about."

Mr. Boomsma's Substitute Teacher Workbook

Your instructor's expectations for today's workshop

Expectations are critical to classroom management!

1.

2.

3.

Your expectations for today's workshop

If you don't know where you are going, how will you know when you get there?

Module One - A day in the life of a professional substitute

Managing expectations

Someone suggested that if a doctor, lawyer, or dentist had 20 people in his office at one time, all of whom had different needs, and some of whom didn't want to be there and were causing trouble, and the doctor, lawyer, or dentist, without assistance, had to treat them all with professional excellence for nine months, then he might have some conception of the classroom teacher's job.

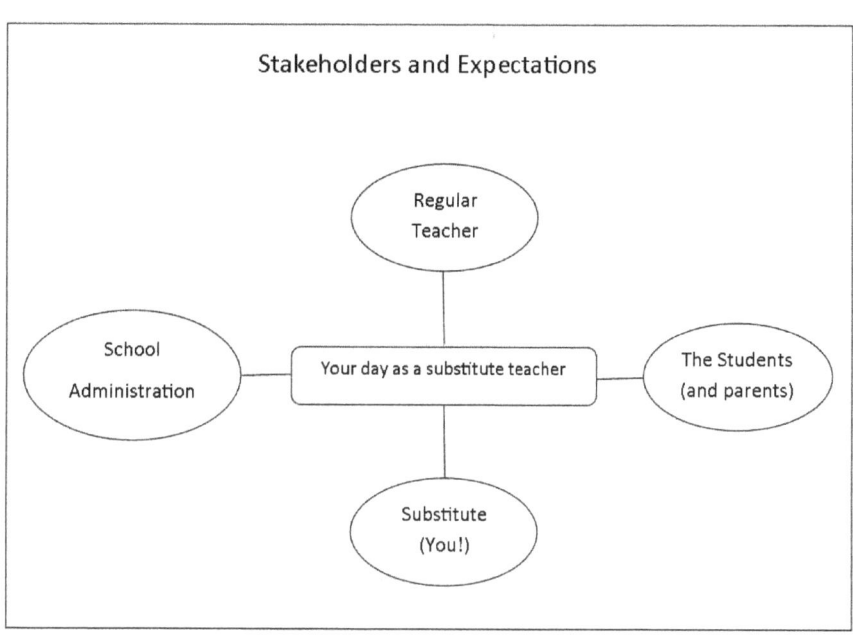

Compounding this, there are multiple stakeholders when it comes to children's education in public school. While all have ultimately the same (or at least similar) goals, all have very different perspectives. Abraham Lincoln is credited with the observation that "Most people are just about as happy as they make up their minds to be." Certainly your day as a substitute has some uncertainty. But giving consideration to the stakeholders and their needs and expectation is a good start to a good day! While it's impossible to please all of the people all of the time, being sensitive to the expectations of those involved will help you manage your day.

The professional substitute's checklist

Checklist management is a proven technique—it works! The sample in your workbook is general; you'll want to add some specific items of your own—and you may develop different lists for different schools.

Mr. Boomsma's Substitute Teacher Workbook

The professional substitute's "sub-pack"

Start listing the items you want to include! Think about how you want to carry it (tote bags work) and plan for it to grow!

Classroom supplies

Post-it notes
_____
_____
_____
_____
_____
_____
_____
_____
_____

Personal items

Clipboard
_____

Business Cards
_____
_____
_____
_____
_____
_____
_____
_____

Module Two - Classroom management

Principle one - behavior is largely a product of its immediate environment

Students tend to behave based on what is happening. Too often we blame behavior on outside factors when we should be concentrating on managing the environment. Our appearance as a substitute for the regular teacher is a change in the environment.

Principle two – behavior is strengthened or weakened by its consequences

Students (just like adults) do what they do because of what they get when they do it. This is both simple and complicated. It' simple in that we are dealing with basic motivational psychology: How much effort a person makes is directly correlated to the anticipated outcome plus how likely that outcome is perceived to be. ("If I do this, then it is very like that will happen.") The complication is that what we think are positive consequences may be negative to another person.

Principle three – Behavior responds better to positive than negative consequences

Human nature is such that we respond better to positive encouragement than punishment. It's one reason there are cheerleaders at sports events!

Principle four – The future determines whether a behavior has been punished or reinforced.

Recalling that consequences can be positive or negative depending on a person's perspective we cannot actually be certain whether we've rewarded or punished behavior until we observe whether the behavior changes in the future.

Every Kid Needs a Champion, Rita Pierson

(This video is embedded on wboomsma.com should you wish to find it again.)

What are two "takeaways" you received from watching?

1.

2.

Note that our workshop attempts to demonstrate what is taught! When showing a video, steps should be taken to ensure students are engaged and listening. Giving the questions that will be asked after watching is one!

Effective Classroom Management Skills

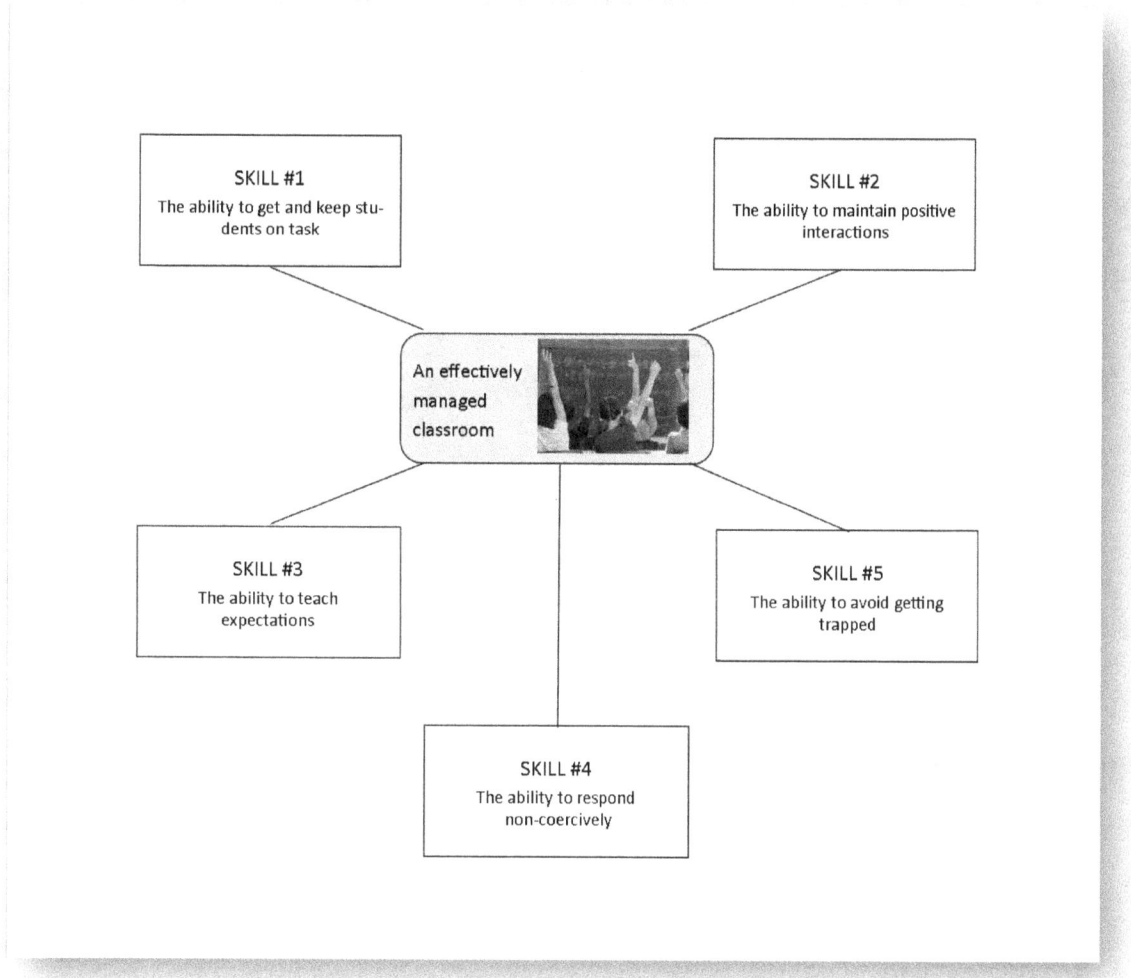

Skill #1 – Getting and keeping students on task

Strategies

Skill #2 – Maintaining a high rate of positive teacher/student interactions

Strategies

Skill #3 – Teaching expectations

Strategies

Skill #4 – Responding non-coercively.

Strategies

Skill #5 – Avoiding traps

Types of traps and avoidance

Other management tips

As unpredictable as a substitute teacher's day may be, there are certain likelihoods. Thinking about some of the challenges you expect, then consider how you will address them.

Anticipated Problem with a student or myself	Planned positive, proactive response
"You can't tell me what to do, you're not my real teacher!"	

Module Three -- Legal considerations and special education

General legal aspects

- Supervision

> Never leave your students unsupervised!

- Due Care

- Release of students

Students should never be allowed to leave the building during the day... nor should you release a child to anyone without express consent of the office!

- Confidentiality

- Records

- Discipline

- Danger

- Technology and social media

Small-town Maine = big-time liability

One of the biggest issues we have concerns about confidentiality. In small-town areas, we often joke or complain about how everybody minds everybody else's business. When it comes to working in school systems, many of the things we like about small-town Maine can create big-time liability for you as a substitute teacher.

> **Under ESRA 2002 (Education Sciences Reform Act of 2002)** all individually identifiable information about students, their families, and their schools, shall remain confidential... Employees, including temporary employees, or other persons who have sworn to observe the limitations imposed by this law, who knowingly publish or communicate any individually identifiable information will be subject to fines of up to $250,000, or up to 5 years in prison, or both (Class E felony).

There are a number of laws involved but we can simplify this greatly by adopting one unwavering principle: "**What happens at school stays at school**." This is actually a simple principle, but it is not always easy to follow—particularly in small-town Maine where we often know each other well and develop a level of comfort and familiarity.

You subbed today in a fifth-grade class. One of the items on the lesson plan was a math test the regular teacher prepared for you to give the class. Sally was the only student to finish the test and she got all the answers right! Sally is so excited she's almost beside herself as she tells you she'd been having a particularly difficult time with fractions.

After school, you stop at the store and a smiling woman approaches you. "I heard you were the substitute teacher in my granddaughter's class today! She was so worried about her math test! How did she do?"

How do you answer grandma's question?

Remember, **what happens at school, stays at school**! You'll of course want to be polite, but you'll need to find a version of this that you are comfortable with:

"I'm sorry, but as a substitute teacher, I'm not allowed by policy to discuss an individual student's performance."

You can, of course, embellish that but you do at some peril. Suggesting Grandma ask Sally is probably okay, but the more you talk, the more liability you are creating for yourself and school.

I've used a positive grade here because people often assume they can't say anything "bad," but it's great to say something "good." Understand our principle is "**what happens at school (good or bad) stays at school**" and it does not just apply to grades. You just need to be a little paranoid and protective of **all individually identifiable information about students, their families, and their schools.** Note also there can be issues within the school. For example, if you walk into the teachers' lounge and a conversation suddenly stops—your colleagues are not being rude; they are protecting you from hearing something you perhaps should not. Similarly, you would not share individual information regarding a student or family with a custodian or cafeteria worker.

Because this is such an important aspect of teaching, consider some situations you may encounter and how you will address them.

Safe schools

Most schools have a Safe Schools Policy that focuses on the behaviors required in maintaining a safe learning environment. It might include expectations of stakeholders—teachers, staff, parents, students and include disciplinary procedures and consequences. What is the substitute's role?

First aid and safety—medications

1. Do not dispense medication of any kind.
2. Refer all injuries (even minor ones) to the office.
3. Carry disposable gloves for your own protection in the event of an emergency involving bodily fluids. Dispose of any used gloves properly.
4. Encourage students to wash their hands prior to eating or after using restrooms.
5. Prevention is the best medicine. Stay with your students. On the playground walk around and scan.

Child abuse reporting

"Any school employee (including substitute teachers) who knows or reasonably believes that a student has been neglected or physically abused shall promptly notify the building principal, nearest peace officer, law enforcement agency, or office of the State Division of Human Services… "[1]

Child abuse is, of course, a serious matter—as is the reporting of it! Substitute teachers must report any suspicion to school administration.

Sexual harassment

Sexual harassment issues are fundamentally the same as in the workplace with the added note that students are a consideration as well as fellow employees.

---

[1] Substitute Teacher Handbook, Utah State University, 2009

Mr. Boomsma's Substitute Teacher Workbook

Evacuations, assemblies, field trips, etc.

These activities are not breaks—you are the teacher and you must assume full responsibility for every student in your class.

Suicide awareness and prevention

LD 609 became law in 2013, requiring a 1-2 hour Suicide Prevention Awareness Education training be completed by all school personnel in each school administrative unit (SAU), island, charter, CTE Region and public school that is not in a school administrative unit. This includes, but is not limited to, administrators, teachers, educational technicians, support staff, custodians, school counselors, school nurses, bus drivers, duty monitors, coaches, food service staff, etc... It is recommended that volunteers working in schools receive training as well. Training needs to be renewed every five years. New hires need to receive awareness education within six months of hire.

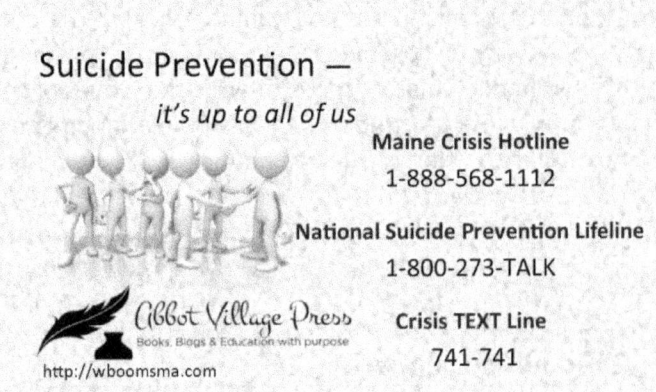

Special education

Substituting in the special education environment can be especially rewarding—and can be especially challenging! Because this is a highly specialized area, this program can only provide a brief overview and several important cautions. One of the good things about substituting in special ed is there is generally a good deal of support and you'll have an opportunity to learn gradually.

One important caution is that you should always be respectful of students involved in special education and treat them with dignity. In fact, it is inappropriate to identify children as "in special education." Confidentiality is extremely important and you must avoid talking about private details regarding a student's disability, behavioral issue, or programs he or she is participating in.

The special education environment is not necessarily apparent to the untrained eye. You may discover, for example

- Classrooms where students with special needs spend part or all of their day.

- Resource rooms where students go for short periods throughout the day, typically for specific topics.
- Special education teachers and paraprofessionals who spend part of their day in different general classrooms, partnering with the teacher but focusing on specific students.

You may be substituting in a "regular" classroom and find special needs students "in and out" of your classroom—since students often know their schedule they will leave and return without any fanfare. This may or may not be listed on your lesson plan and requires some attention on your part—you are responsible for every student all the time.

You may also be substituting in a "regular" classroom and find a paraprofessional (ed tech) in your room. Understand that he or she is there to focus on a particular student or students. He or she will know the other students and may be willing to assist you, but it is important to remember roles. Value his or her experience and be willing to learn, but remember you are the teacher and responsible for the class and achieving the lesson plan.

There is no magic to working with "special needs" students—in part because those needs can be extremely diverse. A detailed explanation is well beyond the scope of this workshop. Whether you substituting as a special needs teacher/ed tech or dealing with a special needs student in your regular classroom, several guidelines to follow include:

1. Offer all students your respect. We use labels to help us understand and cope with special needs, but no student deserves less than your full attention, courtesy, and respect.
2. Some students will simply require more patience than others. Remember "the only behavior you can truly control is your own."
3. Be especially sensitive to confidentiality issues where special needs students are concerned. Watch your language. Students go to a resource room, not a "special class."

Working in this field may initially feel overwhelming, but it can be especially rewarding. New subs may find accepting assignments as an ed tech/paraprofessional a good way to start. You may work with one child throughout the day or work in a resource room where class size is smaller. You'll also have more support than you would "on your own" as a substitute teacher in a regular classroom.

Module Four -- Teaching Strategies

As a substitute, you are expected to follow the lesson plan provided. Sometimes, however, those plans will be very general.

- "Have the students read chapter 5 and answer questions."
- "Complete the first daily five rotation."
- "Bring the students to the rug and read (book) together. Discuss what the story tells us."
- "The students should work on their inquiry project."

Like it or not, you are going to need some basic understanding of learning and teaching skills.

How we learn

An important conclusion we can draw from the Learning Retention Pyramid is that teaching others is generally accepted as having the highest retention rate. Aside from that, there are some controversies regarding its accuracy. Human beings are complex individuals with individual learning style preferences, plus there are too many variables for it to be totally reliable. For example, a well-delivered lecture may be more effective than a poorly written book. That said, the pyramid has some *face validity*—it looks logical!

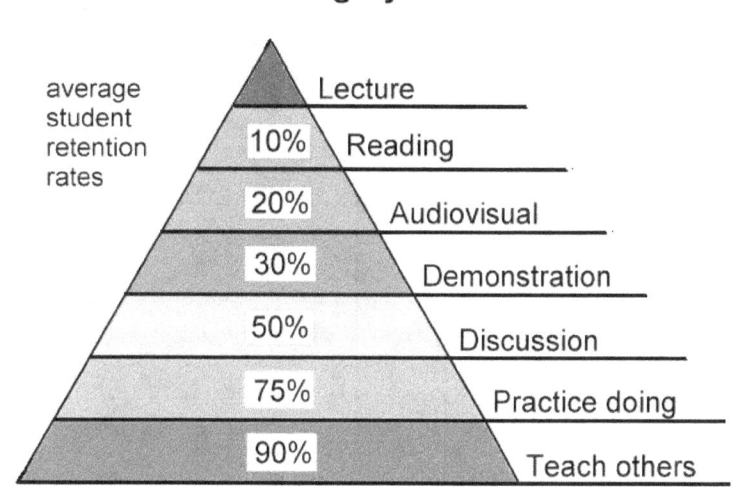

Source: National Training Laboratories, Bethel, Maine

Many of today's classroom activities are based on "teaching others" with students as early as kindergarten having "together" activities designed also to improve social skills. One of the places you will fully appreciate this as a sub is when you are teaching a subject that you are not well versed in.

Think about some examples of how you might rely on the "teach others" approach.

KWL charts

The KWL chart is introduced here because you'll probably hear the acronym frequently and because the concept is also useful for teaching topics you are not familiar with. The chart facilitates self-learning and can be used in a cooperative learning setting. As you develop an understanding of the process and become proficient, you'll find yourself using the logic without drawing the chart.

K – What do I KNOW?	W – What do I WANT to know?	L – What have I LEARNED?

Cooperative learning

In adult education, we often talk about replacing the sage on the stage with the guide on the side. This trend actually started in public education some time ago. Many older adults will remember sitting at desks in rows and listening to the teacher (the sage on the stage) teach. In today's environment, it's more likely that students will be sitting in groups at tables working together while the teacher (the guide on the side) manages the learning process. We've used this in today's workshop!

Basic Steps:

1. Create groups or partnerships
2. State the objective and instructions
3. Create a time frame
4. Assign roles
5. (Optional) Debrief

Questioning

A good general practice when using questions can be remembered as "APC." It stands for "Ask, Pause, Call." If you can prevent the students from calling out the answer you can ask the question, pause so they have time to think about the answer, and then call on a specific student.

Occasionally a lesson plan will indicate "read and discuss." You can manage the discussion with the deliberate use of questions. Remembering the five W's will help you ask varied questions.

- What did the character do?
- Why do you think he did it?
- When did the character decide… go…
- Who was affected the most when…
- Where is the story taking place?

Remember kids are literal. I remember learning this in a very powerful way. I was doing a guest presentation with a class of third graders. Using my best classroom management skills, I reminded them to raise their hands and not call out when I asked the next question. I then asked, "How many people live in the state of Maine?" Every hand shot up. I glanced at the teacher in amazement and asked her, "Wow! Have you just studied this? They all know the answer!"

> I keep six honest serving-men
>   (They taught me all I knew);
> Their names are What and Why and When
>   And How and Where and Who.
> I send them over land and sea,
>   I send them east and west;
> But after they have worked for me,
>   I give them all a rest.
>
> I let them rest from nine till five,
>   For I am busy then,
> As well as breakfast, lunch, and tea,
>   For they are hungry men.
> But different folk have different views;
>   I know a person small—
> She keeps ten million serving-men,
>   Who get no rest at all!
>
> She sends 'em abroad on her own affairs,
>   From the second she opens her eyes—
> One million Hows, two million Wheres,
>   And seven million Whys!
>
> *Rudyard Kipling*

She was chuckling and pointed out they heard me ask "How many (of you) people live in Maine?" and since they each did, they all raised their hands. It was an amusing misunderstanding and I've had to learn to ask the question differently. How would you ask it?

Activity for the teaching strategies module

Choose one activity from the following list and develop a plan for how you will handle it. We will use group learning to complete this activity.

> "Everybody is a genius. But if you judge a fish by its ability to climb a tree, it will live its whole life believing that it is stupid."
>
> *Albert Einstein*

1. The lesson plan says, "As part of our diversity unit, the students should read and discuss [a story or article]." What sorts of questions and points might you use to facilitate the discussion? (Hint: see the section on questioning!)
2. The lesson plan says your class is scheduled for a 45 minute Art Special, but you've been advised Art has been canceled for today. ("Give them a study hall/recess" is not an acceptable answer!) What will you do?
3. Come up with a "freestyle" activity/lesson... a new or different way to teach a familiar subject...
4. The lesson plan calls for you to show a 30-minute film to your seventh-grade class about the Underground Railroad. Describe or list the things you would do before, during, and after the film.

Module Five -- Action Planning

"The more I live, the more I learn. The more I learn, the more I realize, the less I know." — Michel Legrand

Where do you go from here?

K – What do I KNOW as a result of today's class?	W – What more do I WANT to know?	L – What have I LEARNED (Leave blank until you have learned what you want to know in the W column.)

In addition to learning more, there are some specific steps to employment.

List some actions you need to take:

> Visit https://www.identogo.com/ to make your appointment for fingerprinting.

1. Plan to take the required Suicide Awareness and Prevention Class
2.
3.
4.
5.
6.
7.
8.
9.
10.
11.
12.
13.
14.
15.
16.

Resources for further study

Websites

http://www.huffingtonpost.com/lisa-m-dabbs-med/new-teachers-twenty-tips-_b_952949.html is a specific post written in August of 2013 with "twenty tips for new teachers." Many of these tips will be of interest to new substituted teachers. Not everything will apply, of course, but there are lots of clickable links to resources and articles. You'll understand the field of education better and find some opportunities to better yourself.

http://atozteacherstuff.com/ is a teacher-created site designed to help teachers find online resources more quickly and easily. Find lesson plans, thematic units, teacher tips, discussion forums for teachers, downloadable teaching materials & eBooks, printable worksheets and blacklines, emergent reader books, themes, and more.

http://www.proteacher.net/ is geared to teachers but there are forums for substitutes and student teachers.

http://www.educationworld.com/ is a pretty massive site... a good place to visit when you have some time to peruse ideas, tips, sample lesson plans... not specifically designed for substitutes, but if you search that term you'll find some really good stuff! Find the series "In a sub's shoes" for some insights from an experienced sub. Free!

http://nces.ed.gov/statprog/conflaws.asp will review four of the most important Federal Laws regarding confidentiality.

http:// http://www.educationoasis.com/ is a fairly straight-forward site. I like it because there are some great printable teaching aids and they are free and may be reprinted for classroom use.

http://www.edutopia.org is a personal favorite. While the site is definitely aimed at teachers, there are some great articles that subs will find helpful and thought-provoking.

http://www.jokesbykids.com/ can be used for stress relief of to sharpen your classroom humor.

http://myhumor.org/ is a source of "clean humor."

http://wboomsma.com is the instructor's blog of "brain leaks and musings" that includes links to teaching resources.

Remember that your role as a substitute strongly suggests you should be extremely cautious about introducing new concepts, forms, techniques, and practices into the classroom. Your emphasis should be on supporting what is in place.

Websites specific to Special Education

http://www.sensory-processing-disorder.com/

http://www.educationworld.com/special_ed/mild/

http://www.interventioncentral.org/

http://fcrr.org/

http://aspergersyndrome.org/Articles...-Teachers.aspx

http://www.cdc.gov/ncbddd/actearly/ACT/class.html

A Substitute's Checklist

In General...

This checklist assumes this is not your first assignment at the school. Once you have been approved to substitute in a school, you might be invited (if not you can suggest it) to visit the school for an orientation—your opportunity to become familiar with the school's security practices, layout and location of restrooms, and get copies of general information such as the school's handbook. Doing so will help you be prepared and increase your confidence. This checklist is also "wordy" and long with full explanations. You might wish to develop a shorter version for your clipboard.

Before the assignment

- ☐ Be prepared! Compile basic information about the schools where you may be assigned and have it arranged so you can take the appropriate information with you.
- ☐ Assemble a standard "sub pack" that is well-stocked and ready.
- ☐ Organize several clothing outfits that are "ready to go." Comfy shoes are a must!
- ☐ Consider having your own checklist of items you need to address before leaving home so you won't be distracted throughout the day.
- ☐ Leave early enough to arrive at school at least twenty minutes prior to school starting.

When arriving at school

- ☐ Report to the office to sign in and obtain any necessary information. Many schools will have a sub-folder of general information. At a minimum, make sure you have a current roster of children in your class—do any have specific medical concerns or needs? (Sometimes this information will be available in the classroom.) Bear in mind that many of your questions may be answered by information you'll find in the classroom.
- ☐ <u>Understand that the beginning of the day is most hectic for office staff and teachers</u>. Be pleasant, but efficient. Do not expect to have lengthy conversations. You should have most of the general information you need... ask if there is anything special going on this day such as assemblies or field trips, and if there's anything "out of the ordinary."

When arriving in the classroom

- ☐ As you enter, remember to introduce yourself to nearby teachers. This is not the time for lengthy conversations—all of you should be busy getting ready for your day. A good question to ask is, "Is there anything I should know?"
- ☐ Take a slow walk around the perimeter of the classroom noting where things are. Focus especially on any posted evacuation plans and classroom rules.
- ☐ Review the lessons plans and instructions left by the permanent teacher.
- ☐ Make certain your starter activity is ready.
- ☐ Using the lesson plan, locate books, papers, and materials you'll need throughout the day.
- ☐ Study the seating chart or create one if none is available.
- ☐ Write your name on the board. (Do not use cursive below third grade.) You may also list any expectations you have.
- ☐ Your clipboard should include, at a minimum: class roster and count, lesson plans and schedule, any available emergency information.

Mr. Boomsma's Substitute Teacher Workbook

When the students arrive

- ☐ If students arrive at the classroom, stand near the door and greet each child. (In some cases you will be picking the students up from another location.)
- ☐ Without leaving the room, check the hall occasionally to make sure students are putting away their things and getting to class.
- ☐ Encourage the students with reminders that "you know what to do" rather than start bossing them. Create an expectation that today will be no different than any other day.

During the day

- ☐ Keep your clipboard nearby—take it with you to all activities. In the event of an emergency such as a fire drill it is imperative that you have an accurate list of your students. When you take attendance, mark it on your copy of the roster.
- ☐ Keep your interactions with students as positive as practical. You may be bigger, but you are not going to win very many battles in which you are attempting to coerce appropriate behavior.
- ☐ Remind yourself constantly—<u>the only behavior you can truly control in the classroom is your own</u>. Your behavior will determine the type of day you and your students have together.
- ☐ Keep notes of important events and details for your end of the day report to the regular teacher.
- ☐ Be flexible and be prepared to improvise, but also stay on task—you are there to follow the lesson plan.

At the end of the day before students leave

- ☐ Challenge the students to recall the day and, if time permits, ask them about what they learned.
- ☐ Have the students straighten and clean the area around their desks and the classroom in general.
- ☐ Remind the students about their take-home folders and any homework or notes from the office.
- ☐ Provide individual students who were especially helpful with a special thanks.
- ☐ <u>Follow dismissal procedures to the letter</u>. Do not allow students to tell you they have to ride a different bus, go to a friend's house, etc. Do not release a student to a parent or relative without authorization. <u>Refer any controversies or changes to the office</u>.

At the end of the day after students leave

- ☐ Spend a few minutes organizing and stacking papers—use sticky notes to communicate with the regular teacher.
- ☐ Complete or write a report for the regular teacher. This does not have to be an entire journal of the day's events. Note any items on the lesson plan that you didn't fully accomplish. Document any severe behavior problems, but don't make it all negative! Do not leave notes with confidential information just lying on the desk.
- ☐ Close windows, turn off lights, etc. and make sure the room is in good order before you leave.
- ☐ "Check out" at the office, turning in any keys, etc. and thank them for the opportunity.

Sample Lesson Plan

This is an actual lesson plan for a Kindergarten Class… any identifying portions have been removed, thus the white spaces. Frankly, most are not going to be this detailed and thorough!

Friday,
Sub Plans

7:55	Go to the gym and bring back our _____ students. The rest will come as they finish eating breakfast. _____ students are seated on the left-hand side of the back wall in the gym.
8:00-8:10	Students unpack backpacks, sign in for lunch, go to bathroom, sit and read library books at tables. At 8:10 _____ will lead the school in the Flag Salute over the loudspeaker. After they have saluted the flag, ask a student to show you where the Hot/Cold Lunch Graph is. **(They will probably need assistance with this)** Call _____ in the office _____) to report attendance and _____ (Dial _____) to give the lunch count. In case of fire drill: Take the class list that is pinned on the wall beside the door (_____).Exit building by going out the back library door. If you have all students accounted for, hold up green card. If all students are not accounted for, hold up red card. Someone with a walkie-talkie will come help you locate the missing student. **Any notes regarding Bus Changes are placed in the **gray bank pouch** inside the crayon container by the door. **The "Messenger" of the day will take the **gray bank pouch** to the office.
8:10-8:30 All these times are approximate. Don't worry if things take longer or if you get things done more quickly than anticipated.	Calendar time activities: The "Calendar Reporter" will help you. Our bulletin board is too high for them to reach though. *Change date on the calendar. *Change "today is, yesterday was, tomorrow will be". *Put a tally mark for the day's weather. *Days we have been in school: ones, tens, hundreds, and coins for days in school. *Add a coin for how many days we have been in school. *Go over schedule for the day.

8:30-8:45	Have students gather on rug. You can write a morning message on the easel for them to read. **Read Aloud:** Eating the Alphabet **Focus:** We can look at the shape of a letter and say its name.
8:45-9:00 Reading Workshop	**Small Groups: Working with Grammy_____, Read to Self (in library), Working on Writing (in journals), Listening to Reading (on computers)-** Students look at white board to see where they are going. You can wander around room to make sure students are on task. After about 10-15 minutes, ring the bell for students to gather back on the rug.
9:00-9:10	**Whole group: In red pocket chart, sort pictures that have the same ending sound.** Tell students that some words sound the same at the end and we can sort pictures that sound the same at the end.
9:10-9:25	**Small Groups: Working with Grammy_____ Working with _____ Read to Self (in library), Working on Writing (in journals), Listening to Reading (on computers)-** Students look at white board to see where they are going. Rotate cards so students are doing something different. You can wander around room to make sure students are on task. After about 10-15 minutes, ring the bell for students to gather back on the rug.
9:30-9:40	**Recess-** Have students go out into the hallway and gather things from their cubbies. They need to bring everything into the room to get ready for recess. Students put snow pants, coats, boots, hats, and mittens on in our classroom. **This IS your duty.** *If there is an inside recess, _____ class will come to our classroom. Inside recess materials are on bottom shelf of big cupboard (under beta fish).
9:45-10:00	**Small Groups: Working with _____, Read to Self (in library), Working on Writing (in journals), Listening to Reading (on computers)-** Students look at white board to see where they are going. Rotate cards so students are doing something different. You can wander around room to make sure students are on task. After about 10-15 minutes, ring the bell for students to gather back on the rug.

10:00-10:50 Writing Workshop	**Read Aloud/Mentor Text:** Owl Moon Stretch out the most important part. Write about a real life event. (Losing tooth during lunch) (First day of school) (Fire drills) Hand out writing paper. Students will just work on one page for today. Students will focus on writing about something that happened to them. After each student shares and ideas are on easel, students write independently for 15-20 minutes. Walk around room helping students. A small group can work at _____ table with her. *Leave 15 minutes at the end of writing workshop for share time. Choose a few students to share their writing in front of the class.
10:50-11:15	Lunch- Students line up in our classroom and use hand sanitizer in our classroom before going to lunch. At 11:15 students will come back to our hallway to get dressed for recess and return any lunch boxes. Students put snow pants, coats, boots, hats, and mittens on in our classroom.
11:15-11:45	Recess- Walk students outside. **This is NOT your duty.** **If there is inside recess, walk students to _____ room.**
11:45-12:15 Handwriting	Today you will focus only on the **letter c**. Students will only complete page 40 in their orange Handwriting Without Tears work books. Books are on counter under bulletin boards with other handwriting materials. ***Model how to write the letter c before having students complete the page.**
12:15-1:15	**Movement & Music** Bring students to movement (in gym) at 12:15 and pick them up from music at 1:15.
1:15-1:25 Snack	A healthy snack will be delivered to our classroom for all students.

1:25-1:45 Math	**Slate Activities- Activity 4-12** **Whole Group:** Dry erase boards are on blue/green shelf beside easel, along with markers and black socks (for erasers). Students may need to share materials. Clap a certain number of times. Children write how many claps they heard. Hold up a certain number of fingers. Children write that number on their slates. Give clues about a mystery number.
1:45-2:00 Math	**Math prompt:** I had ten snowballs. Three of them melted. How many do I have left? Students can paste prompt on paper and draw an illustration to match prompt. Model how to do this for them. Help them write a number sentence to go along with problem.
2:00-2:15	**Math Read Aloud:** Ten, Nine, Eight
2:15-2:30	Begin packing up. If there is mail to be sent home please make sure students put it in their yellow take-home folders. Students may need help packing up. Please remind students to put their yellow folders in their bags. All snow pants, coats, boots, hats, and mittens get put on in the classroom. They should not be packing up out by their cubbies. *If you need help packing up, please have a student go across the hallway to get Mrs.
2:35 Dismissal	Have the students line up in proper bus order and take the Bus Order list with you to the gym. The bus list is on the green clip board. Walk all students down the hall through 2nd,1st, and K wings. ____ will pick up students who are getting picked up in the K-1 wing. She will have a list of students getting picked up. There are two waves of bus dismissal: one wave of buses leaves at 2:45; the other wave leaves about 10 min. later. When the buses come, you will lead the students outside and make sure they get on the correct bus. The second wave of students remains in the gym while you help load the first wave. Students will sit in the gym on the black line. They know what black line is theirs (black line closest to the door is our class).

"Johnny hit me!"-- a case study

As reported by a substitute teacher (not from this area)...

While substituting a first grade class, I caught two students playing, so I told them I was going to take their names and let the teacher know they were playing while one was supposed to be cleaning up and the other supposed to have been in line, preparing to go to car riders area as part of dismissal. While writing their names the student in line begin to cry (he'd cried an hour before because I pulled his behavior stick). Then he tells me the other student hit him. In response, I tell the student I will be sure to add that in the note to their teacher.

Discussion: <u>Before you read on</u>, discuss what has happened and whether or not you think the substitute has acted appropriately.

Finally, the car riders are dismissed, and maybe five minutes later the principal called me to say that the student's parent is in his office claiming the student was hit with an object and am I aware. I responded that the student did report he was hit, but the never told me the other student used an object. The principal told me to write the student (who did the hitting) up, so I did. I don t understand why I had to write the student up. From what I saw they were both playing and if one is going be written up they both should. Two, in my opinion, the student didn't start crying until I told him I was going to let the teacher know about his failure to stop playing and line up. And lastly, the student never told me he was hit with an object, he only said the other student hit him.

Discussion: <u>Before you read on</u>, do you agree with the substitute's assessment and interpretation of what happened? Do you agree with the principal's decision to write up one student? Why?

The substitute reports the outcome...

A week later, I find out that I can no longer substitute there. I just feel very upset about this situation. What did I do so wrong? They are only kids, no one was hurt. The other student just didn't want to get in trouble.

Turn the page...

"Mr. Boomsma's" comment:

Most schools have a very strict policy regarding hitting, and teachers/subs do not get much latitude in how to handle it—hitting (and threats) must at least be investigated and often must be reported.

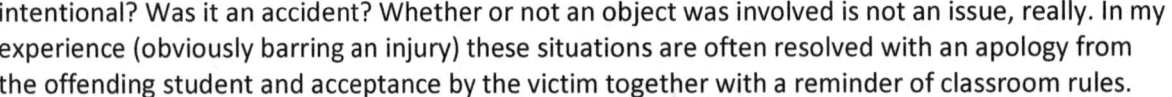

You are correct that the student probably reported the hitting to deflect attention from your threat to report them both to the teacher if I'm following your timeline. But the reason for his report isn't as important as the report itself. A student claiming he or she has been hit does require (in my opinion and often by school policy) some investigation. The investigation need not be long and arduous. Was it intentional? Was it an accident? Whether or not an object was involved is not an issue, really. In my experience (obviously barring an injury) these situations are often resolved with an apology from the offending student and acceptance by the victim together with a reminder of classroom rules.

Note that prior to the principal's involvement, you were unintentionally in the position of writing up two students for "playing" while ignoring a claim of hitting. It's likely that, had you investigated the claim, this could have been resolved quickly. The principal's instruction to write the offending student up was probably damage control because the situation had escalated.

So if anything, there might be an error of omission. It's pretty easy to get caught in these traps because kids are kids. But that's the problem: what we think is trivial can be huge in their minds. I'm not sure why this one incident would result in you not being able to sub there. I'd suggest you attempt a meeting or discussion with the sub coordinator or the principal and ask for some guidance.

Questions and Answers

The following discussions are offered from a forthcoming book "Conversations with Substitute Teachers" by Mr. Boomsma.

Did you ever have a class that you truly didn't like?

I had the good fortune to work for an excellent principal when I started subbing. At the end of one challenging day, I stopped by her office, collapsed in her guest chair and said, "How the heck do you keep doing this every day?"

Her reply has become seared into my brain and heart. "You find something to love about every kid you touch." So simple. Not always so easy--I occasionally asked her about specific kids. "What's to love here?"

What I learned (among many things) is that these kids are just little people who are trying to find their place and their way in a world that can be complex and confusing. In some ways, we have that in common. I'm bigger and a lot older, have a little more experience and insight, but there's still a lot that challenges me and there are times when I'm uncertain of what to do and how to act.

When I think I'm starting to forget that, there's one little guy I remember. I really had trouble "loving" him and so did everyone else, including his teacher. Then I started learning more about him, including how he would sneak off the bus at the wrong stop so he didn't have to go home. And one day he did something truly amazing for me (it's truly a long story or I'd tell it) in spite of the fact he was only in second grade. It became difficult NOT to love him.

I'm the first to admit, it's easier with one than twenty. Yesterday I had two particularly difficult classes... as the saying goes, they really got on my last nerve and I nearly became a teacher even I wouldn't like--out of patience and out of control. But it was the "class" (group) I was unhappy with-- not the kids, really. When I stood near the door for dismissal, I got some hugs and some "high fives" from these little people who are trying to find their way. We'll get another shot at it for sure and maybe we'll all do better.

I'm stressed and discouraged over all the problems I see... what should I do?

I think we can manage stress by deciding how we think about it. A couple of techniques I use...

For me personally, I relabel stress as energy and try to make it a positive. "Thankfully, things aren't the way they should be. That means I have a purpose and work to do."

"Look for the helpers" is one technique I learned to help kids cope during an emergency or traumatic event. It becomes about focus. I don't deny the realities you listed but I try to look at the many other realities.

A third-grader confided to me this week that she could only do one extra activity this year because her Dad said: "that's all we can afford." She spoke very matter-of-factly so we had a nice little discussion about how great it was that she could be so focused.

I know there are many broken adults--some who have contributed to the xenophobia and violence. One of the reasons I continue to be passionate about teaching and kids is "It's easier to build strong adults than it is to fix broken adults." I watch for ANY signs that I might be succeeding.

I also take some comfort in the fact that every generation tends to function quite differently than the previous. I think today's kids have some huge opportunities. Another third-grader made a rather unsolicited impassioned speech to her classmates last week about how important it is that we work together to protect and save our world. (She considers it her mission to pick up any trash she sees on the floor--a nine-year-old environmentalist who does what she can!)

Lastly, it's important to remember we are not our feelings. For several years now, I've been campaigning on this point. "I am sad," is not allowed. "I feel sad," is okay. It sounds crazy at first. How we speak reflects (and contributes to) how we think. How we think largely determines how we feel.

I'm scared because I don't know much about teaching!

You have more teaching experience than you realize. You've spent your entire life explaining things. It'll be easy to be overwhelmed by the vocabulary, acronyms, etc. Put that aside, keep it simple to start.

I like to focus more on learning than teaching. It's more than a semantic difference. I think our jobs are to create enthusiasm and curiosity. We have the advantage (hopefully!) of prepared lesson plans. In a sense, we're salespeople, getting the kids to do the work--ideally with some enthusiasm. Teaching connotates dispensing knowledge. When we focus on learning it can become more of a shared responsibility.

I would suggest you hone your research and study questioning techniques as a teaching tool. I remember once subbing a second-year Spanish Class. Since the kids know me, when we started the class, one of the kids said, "Mr. Boomsma... do you even know Spanish??!" I replied, "No, but I know how to teach it... let's get started."

During that class the I followed the lesson plan that included both individual and partner work. If a kid got stuck, I asked leading questions like "How can we figure that out?" "What's the best way to get started?" "Is there somewhere you can look that up?" "Is there another student that knows this and can help?" "What options do we have?" This wouldn't work if I was a "regular" teacher for an entire semester, but it's a very effective way to get through the day.

I use the same sort of questions with a lot of the crazy math that's being done. I might even admit that I don't know how to do it... let's figure it out together. What would you do first...? I use that even if I know how, because I want them to think! I want them to discover they actually do know how to do it--or can figure it out.

In your research you should stumble on the "APC" questioning method--Ask, Pause, Call. Pause is important... whether one on one or teaching the whole class, don't be afraid of the silence when you pause. Give them time to think! Littles will shoot their hands up before you finish the question, then give a blank stare when you call on them. LOL

Most important. Have fun! I add several classroom rules when I'm subbing... one is "We are going to enjoy learning!"

Bibliography

Geoffrey G. Smith, et al (2009). *Substitute Teacher Handbook.* Logan, Utah: Substitute Teaching Division, STEDI.org.

Cherise Kelley, (2012). *High School Substitute Teacher's Guide: You Can Do This!* published by Cherise Kelley

Dwyer, K., Osher D., and Warger, C. (1998). *Early Warning and Timely Response: A Guide to Safe Schools*, Washington DC, U.S. Department of Education.

Pressman, Barbara L. (2007). *Substitute Teaching from A to Z*, published by McGraw-Hill Companies.

National Forum on Education Statistics. (2006). *Forum Guide to the Privacy of Student Information: A Resource for Schools* (NFES 2006–805). U.S. Department of Education. Washington, DC: National Center for Education Statistics.

Eyster, Richard H., 2010. *Successful Classroom Management*, published by Sourcebooks, Inc., Naperville, Illinois

Kelly, Melissa, (2004). *The New Teacher Book*, published by Adams Media, Avon Massachusetts

Robinson, Ken (2009). *The Element*, published by Penguin Books, London, England

Boomsma, Walter (2013). *Small People-Big Brains: Stories About Simplicity, Exploration and Wonder*, published by Abbot Village Press, Abbot, Maine.

Esquith, Rafe (2007). *Teach Like Your Hair's on Fire: The Methods and Madness Inside Room 56,* published by Penguin Books.

Fay, James/Funk, David (1995). *Teaching with Love and Logic,* published by Love and Logic Press.

About the Instructor

Walter Boomsma has worked in the field of developing individual and organization effectiveness for over forty years. He currently is an adjunct instructor with The Real Estate Learning Group. He also teaches for several adult education programs and is a "battle-tested" substitute school teacher at Piscataquis Community Elementary and Middle School. An active community volunteer, Walter also serves as Communications Director of the Maine State Grange. He is a volunteer "bookworm" with second and third graders and says he "learns a lot" from the stories they read to him and the conversations they have. His book, "*Small People — Big Brains*" details some of his experiences and lessons the kids have taught him.

Books by "Mr. Boomsma"

Unless otherwise noted, books are available from Amazon.com or the Abbot Village Press online store.

Small People – Big Brains

In this book, Mr. Boomsma shares some of his experiences with kids over the past decade as a volunteer and, most recently, substitute elementary school teacher. Many of these short stories will make you laugh. Some will make you cry. All will make you think.

The title of the book comes from an encounter with a young fellow who was firmly convinced that his difficulties at school were the result of his brain being too small. The stories, however, prove that these small people really do have big brains. They just haven't discovered and fully learned how to use them yet.

"This is a light fast read until it isn't, and then you stop and read a sentence or a thought a couple of times… you will enjoy these classic and classy observations on the art and science of learning… a light touch, an entertaining style and some solid content…"

Jack Falvey, frequent contributor to the Wall Street Journal and Barron's

Exploring Traditions—Celebrating the Grange Way of Life

"These essays by Walter Boomsma unpack the teachings of the Grange and relate them to today's world and our everyday lives," writes Betsy Huber, National Master (President) of the Grange. Many people, including Grange members themselves, seem to be wondering about the relevance of this 150-year-old organization in modern society. They may find some answers in Exploring Traditions—Celebrating the Grange Way of Life, a series of essays encouraging readers to understand the basis of Grange ritual and tradition. This is not a "guide to the Grange," it truly is an exploration of some of the words and actions found in the Grange ritual and tradition. Included are the Grange Mission Statement and Declaration of purposes, allowing readers to take away from the book a new and deeper understanding of the Grange—not merely as an historical organization, but also an organization that teaches a way of life that aligns us with nature and creates community.

Betsy Huber, Master (President), The National Grange, Patrons of Husbandry

Words for Thirds Grange Dictionary Program Handbook (planned release, late fall 2019)

The Dictionary Project is a powerful program designed to provide students with their own personal dictionary. This handbook will explore how to start and maximize the benefits of implementing a local program. While the emphasis is on a Grange Program, the techniques and information could be adopted to any civic or community organization that wants to empower students. Includes strategies for implementation, fundraising suggests, presentation outlines, and sample media advisories and press releases. Much of the material is based on the successful program started over ten years ago by Valley Grange. The program has expanded to include four school districts and has distributed over 3,000 dictionaries to date.

Mr. Boomsma's Substitute Teacher Workbook

This workbook was developed for use in "Mr. Boomsma's Substitute Teacher Workshop" and, as such may appear to be missing content if viewed without participating. However, there is plenty of standalone information and valuable resources. It should further be noted that some of the information such as the process for fingerprinting and background checks is specific to the State of Maine. Regulations and processes may differ widely among states and school districts.

The Substitute Teacher Workshop is currently offered by three Adult Education Programs. Additional information is available at http://wboomsma.com.

Conversations with Substitute Teachers (working title, planned release 2020)

Conversations about many of the unique challenges substitute teachers face and how to meet those challenges without tearing your hair out!

Visit Mr. Boomsma's Amazon author page at http://www.amazon.com/-/e/B00JAXUN64.

The Abbot Village Press Online Store can be located at http://abbotvillagepress.com/

www.ingramcontent.com/pod-product-compliance
Lightning Source LLC
Chambersburg PA
CBHW080028130526
44591CB00037B/2712